EDITOR: MARTIN WINDROW

OSPREY MILITARY

MEN-AT-ARMS SERIES 251

MEDIEVAL CHINESE ARMIES 1260-1520

Text by
CHRISTOPHER PEERS
Colour plates by
DAVID SQUE

Published in 1992 by
Osprey Publishing Ltd
59 Grosvenor Street, London W1X 9DA
© Copyright 1992 Osprey Publishing Ltd

ISBN 1 85532 2544

Printed through Bookbuilders Ltd, Hong Kong

Acknowledgements
The author would like to express his particular thanks
for their help and advice to Duncan Head, and Thom
Richardson of the Royal Armouries, HM Tower of
London.

Artist's Note
Readers may care to note that the original paintings
from which the colour plates in this book were
prepared are available for private sale. All
reproduction copyright whatsoever is retained by the
publisher. All enquiries should be addressed to:
  David Sque
  14 Penn Hill Ave
  Lower Parkstone
  Poole
  Dorset BH14 9LZ
The publishers regret that they can enter into no
correspondence upon this matter.

For a catalogue of all books published by Osprey Military
please write to:

**The Marketing Manager,
Consumer Catalogue Department,
Osprey Publishing Ltd,
Michelin House, 81 Fulham Road,
London SW3 6RB**

CHINESE ARMIES

INTRODUCTION

The traditional Western view of Chinese history as a series of cycles, in which dynasties rose and fell against a background of institutions which changed little over the centuries, was to a large extent shared by the Chinese themselves, who liked to base their political systems on idealised precedents dating back to the Golden Age of the Chou dynasty. One of these precedents was for the overthrow, by force if necessary, of a regime which by its failure to guarantee order and prosperity had shown that it no longer possessed the 'mandate of heaven' which entitled it to rule. Another was the essential unity of the Chinese cultural area and the need for a single ruler, the 'One Man' of Chou tradition, to personify this. These two powerful ideas, pulling in different directions, explain why, between the 3rd century BC and the 14th century AD, China did seem to have settled into a pattern in which successive dynasties took power, rose rapidly to a peak of strength and prestige, and then declined into anarchy.

Other factors were the difficulty of maintaining communications and guarding the frontiers in a pre-modern state of that size; and a natural cycle linked to population, which tended to rise in times of peace until it outstripped food supplies and caused unrest. At the beginning of the 10th century AD the T'ang dynasty had collapsed, leaving the country divided among a number of warring states, but this time the reunification of what had come to be thought of as the Empire was long delayed. In the 960s the Sung dynasty established control over the greater part of the country; but during the years of disunity a Manchurian people, the Khitan, had occupied the north-east. Coming under the influence of Chinese culture, they set up their own Liao dynasty, joined in

the 11th century by another 'barbarian' tribe, the Tanguts, who founded the Hsi Hsia state in the north-west.

At this time the Sung were presiding over a period of unprecedented economic and technical progress, but this failed to give them a military advantage over their rivals. In fact, it contributed to the progressive demilitarisation of Chinese society and, combined with an inferiority in cavalry due to the loss of the territories climatically suitable for horse-breeding, helped to force the Sung permanently onto the defensive. Now the alien dynasties provided easy access to the wealthy Sung Empire for the peoples of the Central Asian steppes. Themselves short of manpower and inexperienced at administering a settled economy, the Tanguts and Khitan were relatively unsuccessful at defending themselves against incursions from the north, especially when

Pottery tomb figurines from the Sung dynasty. The figure on the right, representing a guardsman, is the source for a reconstruction in Plate B. (British Museum)

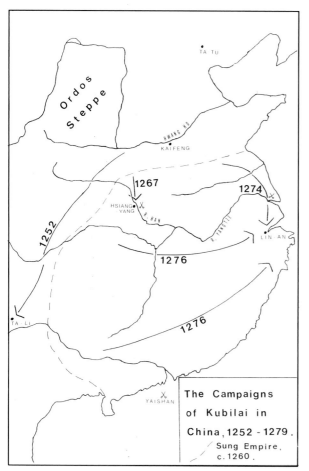

The Campaigns of Kubilai in China, 1252 - 1279.
Sung Empire, c.1260.

Mongols poised on the borders of the Sung Empire.[1]

At this point it should be explained that, dynastic cycles notwithstanding, the China which the new invaders entered was very different from that of previous centuries. In describing it as 'medieval' we intend only to place it within a familiar Western timescale, not to imply that it had much in common with the societies of medieval Europe. In many ways – the size and sophistication of its political units, its industries and urban populations, its reliance on trade and the circulation of money – it almost deserved the title of the world's first 'modern' civilisation. One reason for China's success was its possession of a dynamic frontier in the south. Over millennia the Chinese had spread from their old homeland along the Hwang Ho into the warm and fertile Yangtze valley and beyond, weakly held by aboriginal tribes. Here they found vast new resources, including a crop – rice – which could sustain their civilisation after the ancient wheatlands of the north were exhausted; and a refuge where their northern nomad enemies could not follow them. By the 13th century the centres of population were no longer on the northern plains where every previous dynasty had had its capital, but along the lower Yangtze.

And yet, unlike previous invaders, the Mongols did not remain confined to the north. Just as China had changed, so had the once-backward horse warriors. Led by a succession of able rulers, equipped with siege technology acquired from their settled neighbours, and underpinned by the resources of an empire stretching as far as the Black Sea, they were able to contemplate the conquest of the whole of China. Most significantly, they could recruit thousands of local troops for use against their fellow-countrymen. It may seem strange that Chinese would willingly help to subject the Empire to 'barbarians', but it should be remembered that China had already been divided for generations; the people of the north were used to serving nomad masters, and the weak government of the Sung no longer commanded the 'mandate of heaven'.

The period covered here begins with the accession in 1260 of Kubilai, grandson of Chinggis, as

the skills of their cavalry declined under the influence of easy living. On the other hand, they tended to maintain close relations with nomad tribes beyond their borders and to conduct in their direction the political and technical methods of China.

In 1125 the Jurchen, once vassals of the Liao, overthrew their masters and set up the Kin dynasty, then turned against the Sung. The attack was beaten off, but the Sung were forced to abandon the Hwang Ho valley and retreat to the Yangtze, where their new capital, Lin-an, was founded. Even more quickly than their predecessors, the Kin abandoned their cavalry tactics and came to rely on technology and fortification skills borrowed from the Sung. At the same time their meddling among the nomads of Mongolia provoked the formation there of ever larger confederations. In 1211 the Khan of the newly united Mongols, Chinggis, led them down the by now well-worn road into China. Hsi Hsia was destroyed in 1227, followed in 1235 by the Kin, leaving the

(1) For further details of the Mongols readers should see MAA 105, *The Mongols*.

ruler of the Mongol Empire. Within a few years he was to gain the rest of China and lose the western parts of his realm, in effect giving China unity and independence under an alien dynasty. In 1368 the Mongol Yüan regime was replaced by a native dynasty, the Ming, which survived until its overthrow by the Manchus in 1644. At first sight the two dynasties might seem to have little in common; but in the period under discussion there was a great deal of continuity in military organisation was well as in weapons and armour, while in other ways it stands out as untypical of Chinese history.

The Confucian tradition did not place emphasis on military force, considering that a benevolent ruler should overcome his enemies by persuasion and example. The Mongols were a militaristic society, however, and under their rule Chinese troops were involved in adventures far beyond the traditional boundaries of their world. The first Ming Emperors inherited both the uncharacteristic militarism and the interest in distant lands, campaigning over a wider area than any other native dynasty, and consciously adopting Mongol methods. By the beginning of the 16th century the Ming were reverting to the isolationist and anti-military outlook of the Sung, just at the time that the first seaborne contacts with Europe were introducing new technical advances. Despite its apparently awkward position in the middle of a dynasty, the year 1500 is therefore an appropriate point at which to close a discussion of 'medieval' China.

This Sung painting, depicting a legendary incident from the life of the Emperor Ming-Huang, shows horsemen equipped in a style which changed little between the 10th and 17th centuries. The horse furniture, and the helmet of the man on the far right, are almost identical to those found in the Wu Pei Chih of 1621. (Metropolitan Museum of Art, New York, Rogers Fund, 1941 (41.138))

Sources and conventions

Sources for our knowledge of Yüan and Ming armies are more diverse than for many earlier periods. Archaeology still plays a part, for the Chinese continued to bury their dead with figurines representing guardsmen or military officials, and early firearms still survive in collections both in China and abroad. Armour and other weapons, however, are very rare and bedevilled by the problem of dating, as styles tended to change little. Some Sung, Yüan and Ming period paintings show military subjects, but in many ways more useful are the crude but informative drawings in the military manuals which survive from the Ming. Some of these are reproduced here; they may seem naïve to a modern reader, but I have resisted the temptation to 'improve' them, both because of their intrinsic interest and because of the difficulties involved in their interpretation. The manuals cover not only the appearance but the tactics, organisation and armament of the troops, although unfortunately only short extracts are yet available in translation. The most useful are probably the *Huo Lung Ching* of 1412, a treatise on the use of gunpowder in warfare; *Wu Pei Chih* of 1621, later than our period but incorporating much traditional material; and an updated 1510 edition of the *Wu Ching Tsung Yao* of 1044. The official histories of the dynasties (*Yüan Shih* and *Ming Shih*), compiled from government sources soon after their respective falls, give further details of military affairs; the relevant parts of the former are available in English in Hsiao's *The Military Establishment of the Yüan Dynasty*. The Ming period is covered by many other works, including a biography of the Hung Wu Emperor by

Thought to have been manufactured in north China in the late 13th century, this silver-decorated helmet was probably worn by a Yüan officer. A fabric neckguard, possibly reinforced with internal iron plates, was originally attached. (By permission of the Board of Trustees of the Royal Armouries, HM Tower of London no. XXVIA. 192)

one of his officers; again, these are not available in English, but have been used by the writers of several books, a few of which are listed in the Bibliography. More accessible, if not always reliable, is the *Travels of Marco Polo*, who gives us an eyewitness account of Kubilai's China.

As in the previous volume (MAA 218, *Ancient Chinese Armies, 1500–200 BC*) I have adopted the familiar Wade-Giles system of transliteration for Chinese names, but it may be advisable here to repeat a word of warning: not only are terms often rendered according to different systems, but the same people or places may be referred to in both ancient and modern accounts by quite different names. An Emperor had not only his personal name, but also a posthumous throne–name, and, during the Ming, a reign title. It has become the convention to refer to Yüan Emperors by their Mongolian personal names and to the Ming rulers by their reign titles. Thus, Yüan Shih-Tsu is usually known as Kubilai Khan, while the Ming founder, Chu Yuan-chang, described in posthumous documents as Ming Tai-Tsu, becomes, from his assumption of power in 1368, the Hung Wu Emperor, after the revealing title ('Overwhelming Martial Prowess') which he chose for his own reign.

The situation with city names can be as confusing. I have tried to be consistent in using the names current at the time of which I am writing, so it may be useful to remember that the Yüan capital, Ta-tu, was progressively renamed Pei-ping and Pei-ching (better known as Peking), while Lin-an became Hangchow after the fall of the Sung, and Chin-ling was styled Nan-ching (Nanking) after the Ming adopted it as their capital. Ta-tu was also known during the Yüan period as Khanbaliq, or 'city of the Khan'. Marco Polo uses two separate terms for what we know as China – 'Cathay' for the north, and 'Manzi' for the lands taken by Kubilai from the Sung.

A selection of Chinese weapons, after Wu Pei Chih.

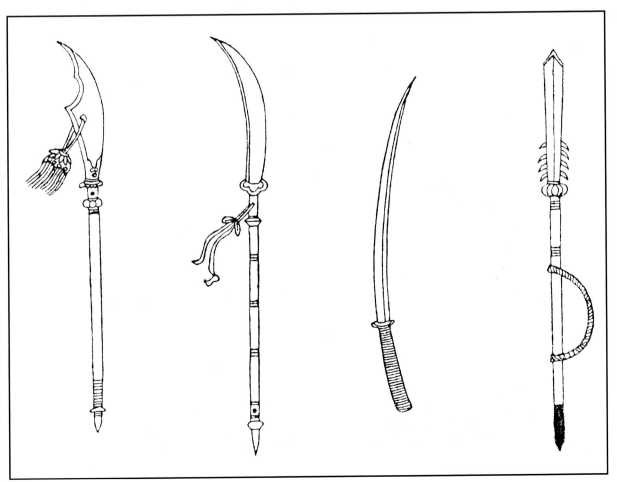

CHRONOLOGY

1260	Accession of Kubilai as Mongol Khan.
1266	Capital of Mongol Empire moved to Ta-tu.
1267–1272	Siege of Hsiang-yang.
1268	Kaidu's revolt. Break-up of Mongol Empire.
1271	Kubilai proclaims the Yüan dynasty.
1276	Fall of Lin-an to the Yüan.
1279	Death of last Sung Emperor. China reunited under Kubilai.
c.1288	Possible date of earliest known handgun.
1294	Death of Kubilai.
1307	Japanese attack Ch'ing-yuan. Beginning of more than two centuries of Japanese seaborne raids.
1332	First known accurately dated cannon.
1351	Outbreak of Red Turban revolt. End of effective Yüan government.
1356–1368	'Ch'un-hsiung' era of 'competing leaders'.
1356	Chu Yuan-chang defeats Yüan at Ts'ai-shih and captures Chin-ling.
1360–1363	Ming–Han war.
1363	Ming defeat Han at Lake P'o-yang.
1365	Ming defeat Wu at Hsin-ch'eng.
1368	Yüan Emperor flees from Ta-tu. Ming dynasty proclaimed by Chu Yuan-chang.
1370	Ming victory over Mongols at Ting-hsi.
1372	General Hsu Ta defeated by Mongols near Karakorum.
1388	Offensive against Mongols resumes with victory at Lake Buyur.
1398	Death of Hung Wu Emperor.
1399–1402	Civil war. Victory of the Prince of Yen.
1405–1433	Seven overseas expeditions under Cheng Ho.
1406–1427	War in Annam.
1410–1424	Yung Lo Emperor's campaigns in Mongolia.
1440–1454	War in Lu-ch'uan.
1448–1449	Revolt in Fukien.
1449	Ming defeated by Mongols at T'u-mu. Cheng-t'ung Emperor captured.
1464	Military reorganisation under Ch'eng-hua Emperor.
1465–1466	Native tribes rebel in Kwangsi.
1465–1476	Ching-hsiang rebellion.
1473–1485	First phase of work on wall system in north-west.
1498	Last expedition to Mongolia under Wang Yueh.
1499–1502	Lolo rebellion in Yunnan.
1513	Arrival of Portuguese under Jorge Alvares.

THE YÜAN DYNASTY

In starting our account with the rise of the Yüan dynasty, we begin in the middle of a long and bitter war. In 1260, when Kubilai came to power, the Mongols had been fighting in China for over forty years; Kubilai himself had commanded armies in the region since 1251, and the year after that consolidated his reputation with a campaign which outflanked the Sung by capturing Ta-li, an independent kingdom in the remote and mountainous south-west. In 1257 he led one of a number of attacks which failed to break through the Sung defences, and in 1259 his brother Mongke, Great Khan of the Mongols, died on the western borders of China. Instead of attending the traditional council to choose a new Khan, Kubilai, who relied heavily on Chinese troops and was increasingly influenced by their culture, had himself proclaimed ruler by his own army at Shang-tu. A rival claimant, Arik Boke, took Mongolia and launched an invasion of north China, but was defeated by Kubilai at Simultu in 1261. For seven years Kubilai therefore ruled, from his base in China, an empire which extended as far as Siberia, Poland and Syria. In 1268, however, another Mongol prince, Kaidu, led a revolt which caused the effective break-up of this vast realm, and although Kubilai remained nominally Great Khan his power in practice extended only over the conquered regions of China and part of Mongolia. In 1271 he proclaimed himself the first Emperor of a new Chinese dynasty, the 'Yüan' or 'Origin'.

Meanwhile, war continued on two fronts. A series of raids and skirmishes with Kaidu's supporters made the Central Asian frontier a perpetual drain on manpower and resources, but the Emperor's first priority remained the completion of his task in China. As early as 1260 he had offered the Sung autonomy if they would recognise him as 'Son of Heaven', and his policy of adopting Chinese culture and encouraging surrender with good treatment is often regarded as an enlightened change from the brutal tradition of his Mongol predecessors. Nevertheless, he could revert to old-fashioned severity if he considered it necessary: 20,000 rebels were executed in one incident in 1281, and according to Marco Polo the entire population of Chang-chow was put to death in retaliation for the murder of some soldiers. However, as the only power which seemed capable of bringing peace to the country the Yüan continued to receive a steady flow of defectors from the Sung.

Kubilai unites China

The war resumed in earnest in 1265, when Kubilai's forces won a major battle at Tiao-yu Shan in Szechwan, capturing warships which became the nucleus of a Yüan river fleet. The twin cities of Hsiang-yang and Fanch'eng, which had denied access via the Han River to the lower Yangtze, fell in 1272, and four years later the Sung capital surrendered to the Mongol general Bayan. Sung diehards fell back towards the east coast, keeping up the struggle from offshore islands; but a fleet under P'u Shou-keng defected to Kubilai, and in March 1279 the Sung navy was defeated at Yaishan. The young Sung Emperor was drowned, and Kubilai found himself the first ruler of a united China since the T'ang.

Yet victory did not bring peace. Apart from the ongoing troubles in Central Asia, the Chinese found themselves embroiled in a series of attempts by Kubilai to extend his rule even further, involving expeditions to Japan (1274 and 1281), Champa and Annam in what is now Vietnam (1283 and 1287), Burma (1275) and Java (1293). None of these was very successful, and most incurred heavy losses from a combination of native resistance, disease and natural disasters. In addition the Yüan had to deal

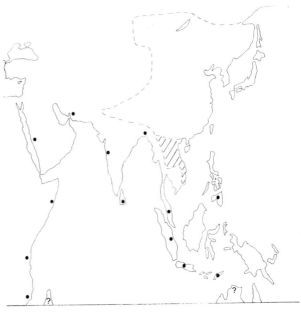

CHINA AND THE OUTSIDE WORLD:

The Yüan Empire, c.1320.

Yüan Vassal States.

• Military Missions of Cheng Ho.

with internal revolts in China, which broke out in many places immediately after the fall of the Sung. Another threat was the revolt of the Mongol Nayan in 1287, requiring the deployment to Manchuria of Chinese as well as Mongol troops. In 1285 Tibet rebelled, not being pacified for five years; even then it remained a source of unrest, requiring constant punitive expeditions as late as 1354. Despite Kubilai's personal moderation his regime was an oppressive one, based on discrimination against the native Chinese; economic mismanagement was rife, combined with a lack of centralised control which enabled dissent to spread. The result was that unlike the Sung, who had kept their troops on the frontiers, the Yüan were forced to use theirs as an army of occupation, stationing units in every province.

After Kubilai's death the overseas ventures ceased, but the northern frontier remained troublesome, while the Chinese underground resistance flourished. In 1308 the government banned the Buddhist White Lotus Society, which subsequently became the most formidable of the secret anti-Mongol groups, and in 1315 the first of a series of major rebellions broke out. Plague (probably imported by Kubilai's armies from Burma), famine and natural disasters added to the regime's problems – census results show a steep decline in population under the Yüan, although it is not clear how much of this was due to tax evasion and the breakdown of authority. The bubonic plague epidemic between 1351 and 1354, however, may have halved the population in some areas; 50 per cent mortality is recorded among troops in the Huai valley. The Mongol élite, always a tiny minority in China, increasingly devoted their energies to feuding with each other, while under a succession of weak Emperors the government continued to pour China's wealth into the Central Asian garrisons and increasing numbers of unproductive Tibetan monks. In 1351 an army of peasants assembled for flood-control work broke out in what became known as the Red Turban revolt, a movement which was not to end until the Yüan were swept from power.

Although illustrating an incident from the career of Mahmud of Ghazni, this picture from Rashid al-Din's World History, made in Ilkhanid, Persia, around 1310, shows warriors in contemporary Mongol armour. It is also one of the best medieval illustrations of the counterweighted trebuchet or 'Hsiang-yang p'ao', introduced into China by the Yüan and operated, as here, by Arab engineers. (Edinburgh University Library, OR Ms. 20)

THE YÜAN ARMY

The Mongol army which proclaimed Kubilai in 1260, and which provided the basis of his power throughout his reign, was in origin a 'Tamma' or Frontier Army, created specifically for the task of conquering China by drafting a proportion of the strength of each Mongol tribe. As was their custom these Mongols fought as mounted archers, but lack of numbers and the unsuitability of this tactic for fighting in the broken terrain and walled cities of China had obliged them to make extensive use of native auxiliaries.

At first the Khan's forces were a conglomeration of private armies led by Mongol princes and local warlords without proper central administration; his efforts to introduce a Chinese-style bureaucracy were at first unpopular with both peoples, but after the rebellion in 1262 of Li T'an, a Shantung warlord, the Chinese commanders were brought under Kubilai's direct control and their troops incorporated into a new formal organisation. The *Yüan Shih* describes the army as made up of four elements: the 'Meng-ku Chun' or Mongol Army was composed of Mongol

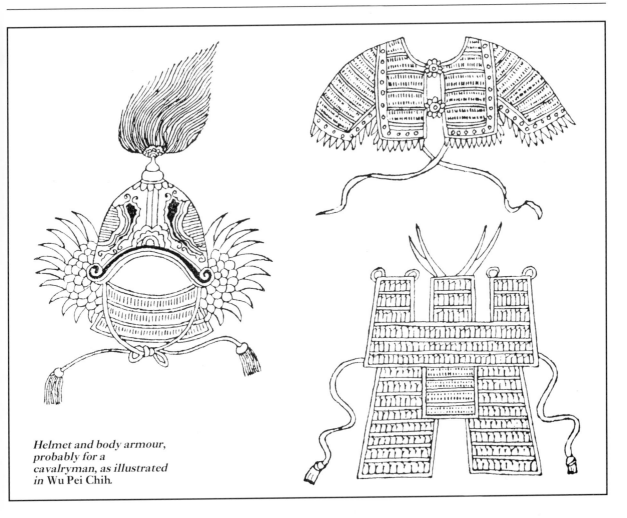

Helmet and body armour, probably for a cavalryman, as illustrated in Wu Pei Chih.

cavalry units under the Emperor's control, in contrast to the 'T'an-ma-ch'ih Chun' or 'Tamma' Army, formed from the followings of semi-independent Mongol lords. The five clans known as the 't'ou-hsia', for example, seem to have fought for the Yüan as allies under their own leaders. Mongol units were theoretically organised according to their traditional decimal system into 'toumans' of 10,000 and 'minghans' of 1,000, commanded by officers with the Chinese titles of 'Wan-hu' and 'Ch'ien-hu' respectively; but in practice Yüan toumans varied in strength between 3,000 and 7,000, being divided into minghans of correspondingly small size. A minghan was further divided into ten companies, each led by a 'Po-hu'. The term 'i', or 'wing', was used under the Yüan and early Ming for a military unit of any size.

All Mongol males between the ages of 15 and 70 were liable to serve, forming a hereditary military caste; but this system, which had worked well on the steppes, was a failure in China. As nomads they had been able to make the transition between peace and war without much difficulty, but to those in China, forced by lack of pasture to become farmers, the call-up caused great hardship. They no longer kept large horse herds and often had to buy animals or arrange to have them requisitioned by the state; China was mostly unsuitable for horse-breeding, and imports from Mongolia and Korea were never sufficient. Therefore by the early 14th century many Mongols could not afford even to travel to join the army, and their military potential was seriously weakened.

The third element of the army was the 'Han Chun', comprising the troops from north China, including not only ethnic Chinese but Khitans, Jurchens, Koreans and Tibetans. Conscription had been introduced in the conquered areas as early as 1235, based on hereditary military families who had to find replacements when soldiers died, but extra mass levies could be raised in emergencies. The troops were organised according to the Mongol system, which in fact had much in common with that of the Jurchens, already in use under the Kin dynasty. Many had originally been cavalry but by the 1260s it was becoming the policy to retain them mainly as infantry, leaving the Mongols to provide the mounted element of the army, and Chinese cavalry units were sometimes ordered to hand over their horses to Mongols.

The captured Sung forces were formed into the fourth element, the 'Hsin-fu Chun' or 'Newly-Adhered Army'. This was almost exclusively infantry and artillery and was regarded as the least reliable part of the armed forces, being placed wherever possible under Mongolian or north Chinese officers. 'Hsin-fu' soldiers were also incorporated into the standard organisation but it is likely that many units in the early period retained the Sung system. A late Sung commentator on the *Sun Tzu* describes a rather idealised table of organisation according to which an 'army' of 3,200 men is made up of two sub-units, each progressively divided into two, down to a 'platoon' of five sections of ten men each. A section consists of two

Detail from a Ming dynasty painting showing a Mongol horse-archer in summer dress. See Plate D for a reconstruction based on this picture. (Victoria and Albert Museum, no. E33-1964)

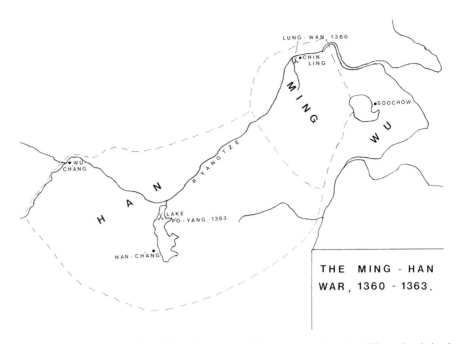

THE MING - HAN
WAR, 1360 - 1363.

squads of five, each made up of a 'pair' and a 'trio'. This suggests that a squad may have contained men with different weapons, perhaps three spearmen and two archers, but another Sung source condemns the practice of mixing up close-combat and missile weapons. Chinese infantry fought with either spears and halberds or bows and crossbows, the bow probably being the most popular weapon. It is significant that when, in 1289, Kubilai wished to make the people of Chiang-nan incapable of further rebellion, he prohibited the possession of bows. Civilians had always been discouraged from using crossbows, and although widely used by regular troops they would have been much less common among peasant rebels.

The Yüan army contained other units, often temporary, which did not fit into this system – e.g. the 'T'ung-shih Chun', Mongol mercenaries captured fighting for the Sung and incorporated into Kubilai's forces in 1279; and the 'Kan-t'ao-lu' or 'looters', independent bands of Chinese which had accompanied the conquerors in search of profit. Notoriously inefficient, these latter discredited the Yüan when defeated, and if victorious ruined conquered provinces by plundering and enslaving the people; in 1274 Kubilai disbanded them and drafted their troops into regular units. Specialist units included the 'P'ao Chun' or 'Artillery Army', and

'Nu Chun' or 'Crossbow Army'. The aboriginal peoples of south China and Ta-li also provided contingents, most of which were used in their home provinces for fear that they might desert if moved far away. The so-called Miao Army, however, raised from other related peoples as well as from the Miao tribe, was used in the Yangtze valley in the 1350s, where it garrisoned the cities of Hangchow and Soochow. Other tribes, particularly the She, were unreliable and often rebelled. Marco Polo describes some of these tribal troops as riding with long stirrups, unlike the Mongols, wearing armour of buffalo hide and fighting with spears, shields and crossbows shooting poisoned bolts. A dozen elephants, or possibly more, were acquired as tribute from Burma, but the only mention of an elephant in battle in a Yüan army is as a mount for Kubilai himself.

The Imperial Guard

Separate from the rest of the army was the 'Su-wei' or Imperial Guard based in the capital, which was not simply a palace bodyguard but the Emperor's private army. Guardsmen, either conscripted or drafted from other units, were regarded as of higher quality than the provincial troops, so that they grew steadily in numbers as the regime came to rely more heavily on them. In 1260 Kubilai's guard numbered 6,500 but by 1352 there were more than 100,000, although

13

The processional ways leading to the tombs of Chinese Emperors were often guarded by large carved figures. This statue, from the tomb of the Hung Wu Emperor (died 1398) near Nanking, represents a military official in armour. (Duncan Head)

This late 14th-century painted scroll illustrates another incident from Chinese legend – the story of Lady Wen Ch'i. Although probably based on a Sung original it is a valuable source for the appearance of steppe cavalry throughout the medieval period: Khitan, Jurchen, Mongol and even some Chinese troops would be very similar. (Metropolitan Museum of Art, Gift of the Dillon Fund, 1973 (1973.120.3))

by then their quality and training had declined and they were beginning to be replaced by Chinese mercenaries. The force was divided into 'wei' or guard units of varying strength, of which 34 were established between 1271 and 1337. Most 'wei' were recruited from a single ethnic group, sometimes Mongols, Manchurians or Koreans, but more often Chinese or 'Se-mu'. The latter term covered troops from the central and western parts of the Mongol Empire, including Kipchaq Turks from the Caspian region, Alans from the Caucasus and even a unit of 'Wo-lo-ssu' or Russians, formed by the Emperor Toq Temur in 1330. The Chinese 'wei' fought as infantry and the others mostly as cavalry; the *Yüan Shih* describes all the guards as 'carrying quivers and bowcases', but this may be an archaic formula for soldiers generally rather than an accurate description. The old Mongol 'Keshig', the bodyguard of the early Khans, survived in Yüan China as a mainly bureaucratic and educational institution, although its members could fight in emergencies.

Yüan generals were conscious of the suitability of the different contingents of the army for different tactical roles, and regularly selected them according to the task in hand. A commander ordered to lead a force in mountainous territory, for example, would request the addition of infantry from the 'Han Chun' to supplement his Mongol horsemen. The 'Hsin-fu' troops were more experienced in naval operations and so were deployed in coastal areas and on overseas expeditions (although the first invasion of Japan in 1274, undertaken before the fall of the Sung, used mostly Mongols, north Chinese and Koreans). Most importantly, the Mongols had to rely on Chinese or Muslim engineers for their siege artillery. Muslims from the west were skilled in this work, but the Yüan seldom trusted them with military command, partly because most were prisoners of war. The 'Newly-Adhered' troops had the advantage of being familiar with gunpowder, already in use in explosive bombs; an accidental explosion in the arsenal at Wei-yang in 1280 was attributed to the employment of inexperienced northerners instead of ex-Sung men. Garrisons were provided mainly by Mongols in the

north and Chinese in the Yangtze delta, while the rest of the south was less firmly held, depending on local levies. On occasion, however, commanders in the south would request Mongol reinforcements if trouble was expected, in the same way as men from the 'Han Chun' would be sent to the coast to stiffen the 'Hsin-fu' units. Garrisons along the frontier with Central Asia and Tibet were mainly Mongolian, supported by non-combatant Chinese agricultural colonists; military-agricultural colonies were set up in many areas, the intention being that the soldiers would save the state the cost of feeding them. Although this did not work well in practice, Kubilai's successful strategy against Kaidu involved denying him the use of advanced grazing grounds in the Ordos Loop of the Hwang Ho by encouraging irrigation and agriculture there.

Wide discrepancies between theoretical and actual strengths of units make it difficult to estimate the total size of the Yüan armed forces, and in fact this information was kept strictly secret at the time, but there can be little doubt that they were very large by

contemporary standards. In Hangchow alone, admittedly the largest city of the Empire and in a region which was particularly tightly controlled, there were 30,000 men stationed, and the total of garrisoned towns and cities ran into hundreds. Expeditionary forces were often between 10,000 and 30,000 strong, but in some cases much larger armies were amassed. Ninety toumans were deployed in China in 1259, and this figure does not include the Chinese troops who probably outnumbered the Mongols. Some 50,000 levies were raised for the siege of Hsiang-yang in 1268, and in 1283 83,600 'Hsin-fu' soldiers were in service. The 360,000 quoted by Marco Polo for the campaign of 1287 could thus be of the correct order of magnitude, but we must bear in mind the logistical problems of moving and supporting such a host in the arid frontier regions. A Ming expedition of 1422, for instance, numbering 235,000 men, required 117,000 wagons and 340,000 pack donkeys, a collection of animals which would have rapidly exhausted the available grazing.

Detail from the Wen Ch'i scroll, showing a group of horsemen on whom the reconstruction in Plate A is based. The armour of the seated officer at far right is coloured gold in the original. The standards are red, blue, yellow, white and black, and the poles black.

This Ming tomb figurine wears an elaborate suit of armour very similar to those of the larger statues at the Imperial tombs; compare Plate H2. (British Museum)

The Yung Lo Emperor and his successors were buried in a massive tomb complex outside Peking; the statues here are later and better preserved than those from Nanking, but show similar styles of armour. See Plate H for a reconstruction from this source. (Su Evans & Richard Patching)

This early 15th-century presentation sword, probably preserved in a Tibetan monastery, is a rare surviving example of the Ming armourer's art. The hilt is gilded, and the scabbard of wood covered in green leather and lined with red silk. (The Board of Trustees of the Royal Armouries no. XXVIS. 295)

THE CIVIL WARS, 1351–1368

In 1351 prophecies of the return of a descendant of the Sung Emperors spread by the White Lotus Society encouraged the growth of the anti-Yüan Red Turban movement out of the co-operation of several insurgent peasant armies. In the following year the rebels defeated the Miao Army at I-feng Bridge, but were unable to dislodge it from Hangchow, and so turned their attention to the north. They made several incursions into the Hwang Ho plain between 1352 and 1359, at one point taking K'aifeng and proclaiming a restored Sung dynasty. Much of the early success of the rebels was due to the Yüan's failure to maintain city walls, or even to repair the breaches made in their own conquest 80 years earlier – a reflection of their contempt for fortification and mistrust of the urban populace. The government, weakened by internal dissension, was more than once on the verge of crushing the rebels but abandoned the campaign without achieving final victory. Mongol warlords set up their own virtually independent states; and although the Red Turbans were eventually suppressed in 1363, they had distracted the Yüan long enough to ensure that it would never regain its grip on the south. In the Yangtze valley, as central authority collapsed, rebel armies and the forces of local officials set up a number of independent states. Most important of these were a revived 'Sung Empire' at Hanyang in the south-west, Chou in the far south, Wu on the coast south of the lower Yangtze and Han on the middle reaches of that river. Sandwiched between the latter two were the lands of Kuo Tzu-hsing, one of the original Red Turban leaders.

Kuo died in 1355 and was succeeded by Chu Yuan-chang, who had once been a beggar but had risen quickly through the ranks of Kuo's army. Early in the following year Chu defeated a Yüan river fleet at Ts'ai-shih and took the city of Chin-ling, which he fortified as a base. He then fought several battles with the Miao Army but failed to take Hangchow, which fell to his more powerful neighbour, Chang Shih-cheng of Wu. By 1360 the Yüan had been driven out of the lower Yangtze valley and Chu found himself surrounded by his fellow warlords, who were mostly content to hold the territories they had taken. This enabled Chu to build up his forces in peace, and to pursue a policy of appealing to the common people by storing grain for famine relief and forbidding his troops to plunder. Soon he felt strong enough to take on his rivals.

It is surprising to find that the armies of these rebel states had quickly attained a high level of sophistication. Although short of cavalry they were far from mere peasant mobs, and deployed massive fleets of ships and hundreds of artillery pieces, including cannon. Much of this material was taken over from Yüan units, but even so it suggests that the country had not been as ruined economically as is often thought. The reasons for the success of Chu's forces, however, lie not in superior technology but in superior leadership, and in particular the strict discipline of the army.

The Ming–Han War

In 1360 the more populous kingdom of Han under Ch'en Yu-liang, which dominated the Yangtze with a fleet of several hundred ships, woke up to the threat posed by Chu and moved to eliminate him. The ensuing conflict is usually known as the Ming–Han War, although strictly speaking it is anachronistic to refer to Chu's state as the Ming, a title it did not take until later. The Han attempted to take Chin-ling by an amphibious assault but were defeated at Lung-wan; in the following year, using ships captured in the battle, the Ming won another victory on the Yangtze. Early in 1363 Ch'en raised an army, allegedly of 600,000 men, and sent it down the river in a new fleet of enormous warships (described by their awestruck enemies as 'like mountains') to besiege Nan-ch'ang on Lake P'o-yang. A Ming army of 100,000 sailed to raise the siege, defeating the Han in a decisive battle on the lake by the use of fireships and superior mobility. Naval warfare is unfortunately outside the scope of this book, but it is interesting to note that the fleets deployed very much as if for a land battle, with the largest ships in the centre and the lighter and faster vessels on the wings; and that the Han tried to close with and board the smaller Ming craft, relying on hand-to-hand fighting and close-range missiles. At the end of the battle Ch'en was killed by an arrow, and in the following year his son surrendered to Chu.

Chang Shih-cheng of Wu, who had foolishly refused an alliance with Han, was the next victim. In 1365 his army was broken by a Ming cavalry charge at the relief of Hsin-ch'eng, and in October 1367 his capital, Soochow, fell after a ten-month siege; 250,000 Wu troops were drafted into the Ming army. A month later Chu ordered the simultaneous conquest of the rest of China. A fleet sailed down the coast and up the Si River, receiving the surrender of the states of Sung and Chou, while the general Hsu Ta led 250,000 men in a two-pronged attack on K'aifeng. By now the Yüan were in complete disarray; and in September 1368, almost unopposed, Hsu entered Ta-tu, now renamed Pei-ping ('The North is Pacified'). The Emperor Toghon Temur fled back to Mongolia, and Chu Yuan-chang was proclaimed the first Emperor of the 'Ming', or 'Brilliant' dynasty. It is symptomatic of the shift of wealth and power from north to south during the medieval period that, for the first time in Chinese history, a power based in the Yangtze valley had been able to unify the country, reversing the north's political dominance.

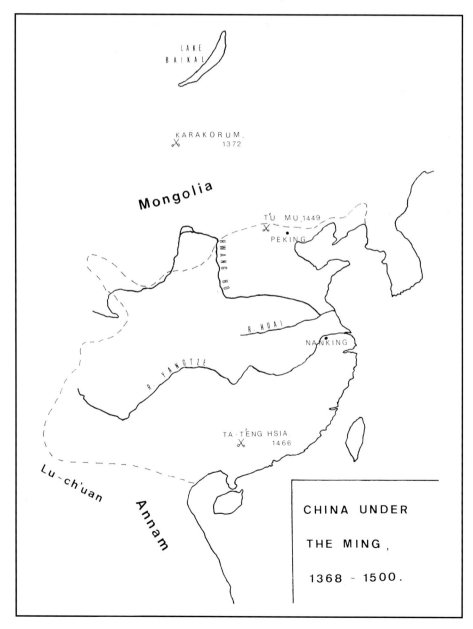

LAKE BAIKAL

KARAKORUM, 1372

Mongolia

HWANG HO

TU MU 1449

PEKING

R. HUAI

NANKING

R. YANGTZE

TA-TENG HSIA 1466

Lu-ch'uan

Annam

CHINA UNDER THE MING, 1368 - 1500.

THE MING DYNASTY

The capture of Ta-tu did not bring the war to an end, as while the Yüan Emperor and many of his Mongol followers had escaped, remaining a threat to China's northern provinces, the new regime was determined to take over the whole of the Yüan Empire including the Central Asian provinces. Shensi and Kansu in the north-west were secured after a victory over a Mongol army at Ting-hsi in 1370, and in the following year the Shu state in Szechwan was conquered; but in 1372 an army under Hsu Ta was decisively beaten in Mongolia near Karakorum. This ended the Ming dream of ruling a steppe empire; but security on the northern frontier continued to be maintained by an aggressive policy, with fortified garrisons pushed well forward beyond the boundary of settled agriculture. The strategic key to the security of north China against nomad invasion was the Ordos Steppe, in the great northward loop of the Hwang Ho; and, just as Kubilai had done, the new Emperor denied it to his enemies by encouraging

irrigation projects to make it suitable for settlement by Chinese. In 1387 the expeditions into Mongolia resumed, culminating in a battle at Lake Buyur in which the Ming general Lan Yu trapped a nomad army against the shore of the lake and annihilated it, but in 1398 the death of the Emperor brought the northern war once again to a temporary halt.

The Hung Wu Emperor's strong centralised rule had been in many ways a blessing for China, despite

The rarely seen rear view of this statue shows clearly how the armour was fitted and worn. (Duncan Head)

Detail of the sword hilt and scabbard fittings of one of the statues from Peking. (Duncan Head)

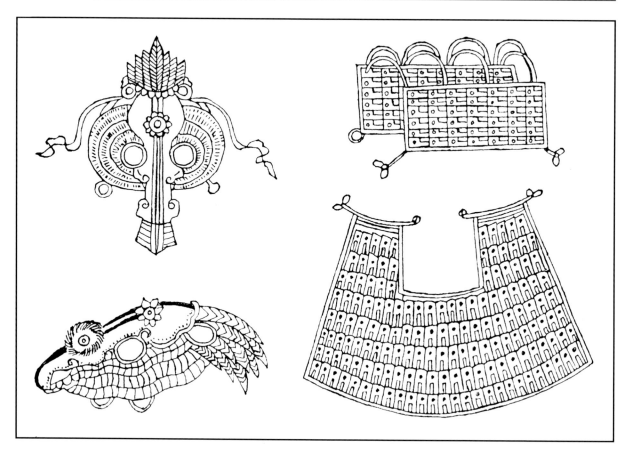

Chamfrons and horse armour from Wu Pei Chih. *Although illustrated in the manuals, horse armour was probably never very common among ethnic Chinese cavalry.*

the paranoia which marred his later years; but he had made the mistake of granting huge semi-independent fiefs to his relatives, the Imperial Princes, and permitting them to raise private armies. The result was civil war on his death; the throne passed to his grandson, the cultured and unwarlike Chien-wen Emperor, who was soon challenged by his uncle, the Prince of Yen. At this time the Ming capital was still at Chin-ling, now Nanking, while the Prince's power base was in the north around Pei-ping, so most of the fighting was concentrated on the plain between the Hwang Ho and Yangtze, and in particular the vital Grand Canal by which grain was transported to the north.

The rebel army began with about 100,000 men, a third of the strength of the Imperial forces, but the northerners were stronger in cavalry and more accustomed to the harsh winters of this theatre than those from the south. On the other hand the Emperor seems at first to have had a monopoly of gunpowder weapons. In May 1400 the Prince won a victory at Pao-ting, but for nearly two years the struggle swayed back and forth along the Canal. Then in January 1402 the Prince, employing large numbers of Mongol horsemen, advanced on Nanking. Although beaten several times in the field he repeatedly out-manoeuvred his opponents, helped by the Emperor's mistrust of his best general, Hsu Hui-tsu. In June the rebels reached the Yangtze and crossed with the aid of a defecting Imperial fleet; a month later the gates of Nanking were opened by sympathisers and the city was taken after fierce street-fighting, in which the Emperor was killed. The Prince, ascending the throne as the Yung Lo Emperor, quickly restored the aggressive policies of the Hung Wu reign, beginning with a brutal purge of his opponents in which thousands died.

One of the first acts of the new ruler was to move the capital to Pei-ping, once again renamed Peking ('Northern Capital'). This placed him nearer the vital northern frontier, but involved the Empire in enormous disruption and expense, the necessary fortification work dragging on into the 1440s. He rewarded his supporters by creating a new military aristocracy, but did not allow them to raise their own armies or to forge close links with individual units by remaining too long in one place. The fiefs of the Imperial Princes were abolished.

At first the aim was to secure peace in the north by diplomacy, settling loyal Mongol tribes within the Empire to form a buffer zone, and the garrisons on the steppe were pulled back to more defensible positions. At the same time a policy of expansion was adopted in the south; Annam was invaded in 1406 and turned into a province, but the natives carried on a guerrilla war which drained Chinese resources and led to several defeats before the province was abandoned in 1427. Between 1405 and 1433 the eunuch Cheng Ho was sent on seven long-distance sea voyages with fleets said to have carried as many as 70,000 men. The aim was diplomatic rather than military, but Ming forces did intervene in succession disputes in Java, Sumatra and Ceylon. States on the Malay Peninsula and in Indonesia accepted nominal Chinese overlordship, and on his longest voyage Cheng Ho crossed the Indian Ocean to the coasts of Arabia and Africa.

The north was not at peace for long, however, as a new tribal grouping, the Oirat Mongols, began to launch raids from beyond the settled buffer zone. The Emperor personally led five expeditions into Mongolia between 1410 and 1424 with the intention of breaking up the Mongol confederation and punishing the raiders; all won battles, but none was decisive due to the difficulty of pursuing the mobile horsemen. On the last campaign the Yung Lo Emperor died, bringing to a close this new phase of offensive warfare.

Ming decline

After the Yung Lo reign, although the Empire remained a formidable military power, the numbers and efficiency of Ming armies began to decline. The story of this decline is often repeated in discussions of the Ming, but for our period at least it should not be over-emphasised; Chinese forces were on balance successful against their enemies until a defensive mentality really took hold from the 1540s onwards. The main problems were cultural and economic.

Chinese society had drifted away from warlike pursuits under the Sung, and the military ethos of the early Ming Emperors was not shared by most of their educated subjects. Troops had therefore to be raised by forming families into an hereditary military caste

Drilling with the two-handed sword, after Wu Pei Chih.

Restored in the same style as the 15th-century original, the impressive architecture of the

Forbidden City in Peking illustrates the style of early Ming building. (Su Evans & Richard Patching)

with an obligation to serve; unlike the feudal obligation of the European nobility this carried little social status, often involved great hardship, and was evaded where possible. Chinese generals had long been accustomed to use their men as labourers when not on campaign, which was detrimental to morale. This situation was made worse by the environment in which many units were deployed, for while the Yüan had been prepared to tax China to support the garrisons on the steppe, the Ming Emperors were determined to make them pay for themselves as agricultural colonies. This, through a combination of the harsh climate and the inexperience of the men, never worked properly, and eventually incentives had to be introduced to persuade merchants to send grain to the frontier. Isolated and often starving, the men deserted in growing numbers, while their officers kept false records in order to embezzle the rations. By the late 15th century units were regularly found to be at half strength or less, and mercenaries had to be hired to supplement the regulars. No Chinese dynasty could ever afford enough mercenaries to guard its enormous borders, and a series of financial crises further weakened the army. In the 1440s natural disasters added to the burden, in particular the disastrous flooding of the Hwang Ho in 1448; and major rebellions began to break out in the south. From then on the main military preoccupation of the dynasty, apart from the ever-threatening Mongols, was the maintenance of order in China itself.

In the same period, however, trouble on the south-western border, in Yunnan, led to a series of campaigns in which local Chinese forces took the offensive once more. The Shan people of Lu-ch'uan raided Yunnan and in 1440 defeated a punitive expedition. The local governor, Wang Chen, formed an alliance with the rival Burmese states of Ava and Hsien-wi and thrust repeatedly into the tropical forests as far as the west bank of the River Irrawaddy. This was successful in protecting Yunnan, but was to have an unfortunate result in another theatre.

In July 1449 the Oirats under Esen Khan launched a major offensive in the north and Wang Chen, now at the court in Peking, persuaded the Cheng-t'ung Emperor to lead a counterattack, with Wang as military commander. Wang's inexperience in steppe warfare led to a disastrous defeat at T'u-mu which plunged the country into temporary chaos.

Cavalry of the Yuan period, c. 1260
1: Mongol heavy cavalryman
2: Chinese cavalryman

A

Chinese troops of the Yuan, c. 1280
1: Guardsman
2: Crossbowman
3: Infantryman

B

Southern auxiliaries of the Yuan, c. 1300
1: Fukienese tribesman
2: Military official
3: Southern pirate

C

The Red Turban Revolt, c. 1350
1: Mongol Trooper
2: Red Turban rebel

D

Ming troops, c. 1400
1: Halberdier
2: Standard bearer
3: Handgunner

大
明

王

Rocket-launcher, c. 1450

F

Ming elite troops, c. 1500
1: Cavalry trooper
2: Rocketeer
3 & 4: Drummers

G

Ming commander and staff, c. 1500
1: Civilian official
2: Ming general
3: Standard bearer

H

Worst of all, control of the Ordos region was permanently lost to the nomads.

A major reorganisation in 1464 restored some of the efficiency of the army, but the days of large-scale offensive action were over. Henceforth the government was to fluctuate between a policy of punishing the Mongols with small, fast-moving cavalry columns, as advocated by the scholar-turned-general Wang Yueh, and an entirely defensive one involving the building of walls to pen them up in the Ordos Loop. Proposals for another offensive to occupy the Ordos were still sometimes considered and once, in 1472, actually set in motion, but each time financial worries and the caution of the generals caused them to be abandoned. The Oirat confederation broke up soon after their victory in 1449, but by prohibiting trade with Mongolia the Chinese missed an opportunity to make a lasting peace. By now the tribes had become dependent on Chinese goods and livestock, and were forced to continue raiding in order to obtain them.

In 1473 work began on a system of walls in Shensi Province requiring months of labour by 40,000 troops; between then and 1485 nearly 600 miles of rammed earth walls were built, overlooked by watch-towers and anchored on fortified towns, and in 1482 they passed their first important test when a Mongol army became bogged down among the defences and was forced to abandon an attack into China. It is worth mentioning at this point that there had been no Great Wall along the frontier under the Yüan and

Another view of the Forbidden City. The construction of this palace and the surrounding fortifications strained the resources even of the Ming Empire. (Su Evans & Richard Patching)

early Ming. The original Ch'in wall had long since fallen into ruins and although subsequent dynasties, notably the Han and the Kin, had built walls, they had been far to the north of the Ming frontier and in any case had been so completely neglected that few traces had survived. In our period the Ming system covered only the Ordos region in the north-west, the eastern sections dating from the 1540s and later.

Of the internal revolts which plagued the Ming in the 15th century the worst was the Ching-hsiang Rebellion of 1465 to 1476, based on the area west of the Han River around the old fortress of Hsiang-yang. In Sung times this had been a very rich and populous district, but it was depopulated during the Mongol conquest, and in Ming times formed a sort of internal 'frontier region' where central control was weak and bandits flourished. The first serious outbreak was crushed in 1466; but four years later a charismatic leader known as the 'T'ai-p'ing Wang' or 'Prince of Great Peace' again raised a rebel army, which took six years and 250,000 men to suppress. Other sources of trouble were the tribes of the south, especially the Miao, Yao and Lolo, who resented the appropriation of their lands by Chinese settlers.

For the majority of subjects of the Ming, however, the 14th century was a period of peace, accelerating the decline of the army. The new policy

33

of aggression in Mongolia died with Wang Yueh in 1499; until the previous year, at the age of 71, he had still been in the habit of leading his cavalry raids in person. In 1504, when the Hung-chih Emperor announced his intention of leading another expedition northwards, his ministers united in dissuading him, admitting that the army was far inferior to that of the Yung Lo period. Within a few years the arrival of the Portuguese off the southern coast was to mark the end of China's long period of independent military development.

THE MING ARMY

Until the end of the Ming–Han War in 1363 Chu's army consisted of various separate contingents, many taken over intact from the Yüan or rival warlords, under their own leaders. Units of the Miao Army were incorporated in this way after 1360. In 1364, however, a major reorganisation broke up the existing units and redistributed them into 'wei', or brigades, of 5,000 each, divided into five battalions, 'chien-hu

so', each of ten 'po-hu so'. Independent battalions, 'shou-yu', each 1,000 strong, also existed. The influence of the Yüan system is obvious. After 1368 this was regularised into the 'wei-so' system, under which units corresponded to military districts where they were stationed, and combined with the 't'un-t'ien' or military colonies. Up to four-fifths of the soldiers grew food to support the remainder, who were responsible for guard duties. At first this worked acceptably, as the wars had left large regions of underpopulated land which could be settled; but as population pressure grew and military necessity forced the troops to concentrate in arid regions it broke down, with the results discussed above. There were about 500 'wei' throughout the Empire, each nominally 5,600 strong, giving a total of between two and three million hereditary troops, but they gradually fell below their theoretical numbers until by the late 15th century most were below half strength. Additional to these were the guards units stationed around the capital, and the generally better equipped garrisons of the fortified cities on the northern frontier.

Guard units fell into three groups. The 'Ch'in

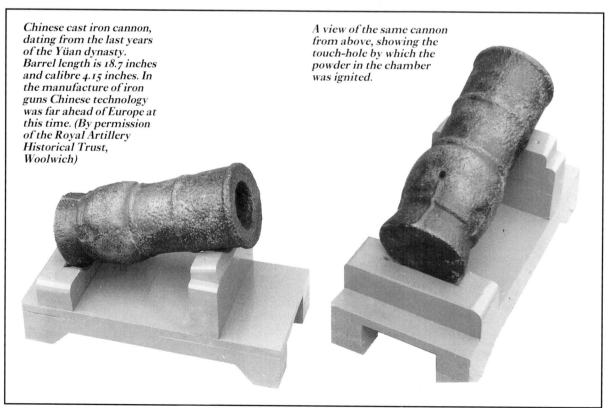

Chinese cast iron cannon, dating from the last years of the Yüan dynasty. Barrel length is 18.7 inches and calibre 4.15 inches. In the manufacture of iron guns Chinese technology was far ahead of Europe at this time. (By permission of the Royal Artillery Historical Trust, Woolwich)

A view of the same cannon from above, showing the touch-hole by which the powder in the chamber was ignited.

chun wei', like the Yüan Keshig, was a bureaucratic organisation comprising the Emperor's personal bodyguard and the secret police. The 'Hu-wei' or 'Princely Guards' came under the control of the Imperial Princes and were disbanded by the Yung Lo Emperor early in the 15th century. This left the 'Ching-wei', eventually consisting of 72 units making up the 'Ching Chun' or Imperial Army. This provided the core of all major expeditions until 1449, when it was lost at T'u-mu. It was later re-formed, but no longer as an élite force – in fact it was employed so rarely that it became ineffective. By 1504 the guards had declined so far that a minister argued against sending them to reinforce the border garrisons on the grounds that they would run away and demoralise those whom they had been sent to help. As early as 1434 volunteers had been hired to supplement the hereditary troops, and after 1449 these mercenaries came to bear the brunt of the wars against the Mongols and internal rebels. Many were in fact Mongols themselves, greatly valued for their traditional cavalry skills. The native Chinese mercenaries, however, were usually recruited from criminals and vagabonds and were noted for their resistance to discipline. Conscripted militia were also used in the crisis of 1449 when the Oirats threatened Peking, and called up on occasion thereafter, although the practice was not placed on a legal basis until 1494.

In the Hung Wu period there was little difficulty in finding large numbers of experienced soldiers in a country militarised by the long series of wars, but savage discipline was needed to ensure that hereditary officers trained their sons to succeed them: at least one man had his nose cut off when his son was discovered playing the flute instead of working at his military exercises. This system was regularised in the Yung Lo reign by the establishment in Peking of three 'ying' or training camps, to which troops were sent in rotation. The 'Wu-chun ying' drilled recruits and specialised in infantry manoeuvres; the 'San-ch'ien ying' employed Mongol instructors to teach cavalry warfare, scouting and signalling; and the 'Shen-chi ying' trained men in the use of firearms. (Surprisingly, in the country which had invented gunpowder, many Annamese gunnery instructors were imported.) There was also a horse training camp where army mounts were broken in by Mongols. Several times this system fell into decline and was

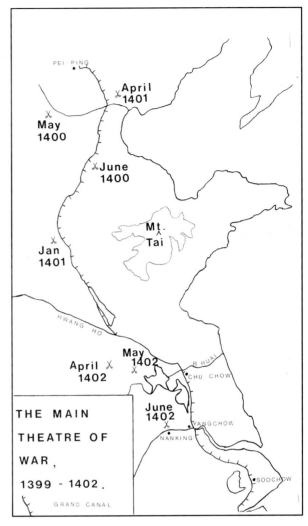

THE MAIN THEATRE OF WAR, 1399 - 1402.

revived, notably in 1464 when twelve units were set up under a veteran general to train infantry, cavalry and artillery together in combined-arms tactics.

Despite the sophistication of the training programme, however, it failed to produce enough high-ranking officers of ability and experience. Military examinations were set up in parallel with the civil service ones, but the low status of the army did not attract the required calibre of applicants. Inevitably the descendants of hereditary commanders were of much more mixed ability than the original appointees had been, and officers of lower rank were selected mainly for their physical strength and skill at archery, so lacked potential for promotion. After the Yung Lo period the Emperors tended to live very sheltered lives at court, and so were not able or inclined to supervise the army personally; military affairs were left to the bureaucrats of the Board of War, who regarded the generals as their social inferiors and often suspected the able ones of disloyalty. The last Emperor to take the field himself was Hsuan-te, who in 1428 personally killed several Mongols. Other sources of generals were court eunuchs and the scholar gentry, who could on rare occasions produce a commander of the calibre of Wang Yueh.

Many non-Chinese troops were still used by the Ming. Mongols, either those remaining in China after the fall of the Yüan or from allied tribes along the frontier, were employed in most Ming armies. The success of the Prince of Yen in 1402 was largely attributable to his 100,000 Mongol cavalry, while smaller numbers could be found serving even in the far south. Armies in Central Asia, like those sent to Hami in 1473 and 1495, could consist almost entirely of Mongols. Like the Yüan the Ming used contingents from the southern tribes in regions close to their homelands, when possible setting one tribe against another. In the Burmese campaigns the states of Ava and Hsien-wi provided allies, probably including elephants (which were certainly used by Ava in an earlier invasion of China), but again these were only used in close proximity to their areas of origin. It was considered undesirable to deploy northerners in the south and vice versa, but in the case of Chinese troops it was not always possible to avoid this.

By the mid-14th century firearms were in use in considerable numbers – they were instrumental in the defeat of the state of Shu in 1371, and in 1388 an army including 2,000 handgunners was sent to crush an Ava invasion. At about this time the first field pieces on wheeled carriages also appeared. In 1412 the Emperor ordered five cannon to be set up on mountain passes near Peking, many other strategic sites being so protected by the 1440s; in one year, 1465, 300 large bronze cannon were manufactured. But these figures can give a misleading impression, as production was restricted for security reasons to the capital, and elsewhere firearm-equipped troops were a very small minority, most infantry still relying on bows, crossbows, swords and the huge variety of pole weapons illustrated in the manuals. The cavalry, whether Mongol or Chinese, were mostly mounted archers.

Types of 15th-century Chinese artillery, as illustrated in Huo Lung Ching.

MILITARY TECHNOLOGY

It was inevitable that a society as advanced as China should have looked to technology for the solution of its military problems, and as early as the Han dynasty we find victories over the barbarians attributed to possession of inventions like the **crossbow**. This weapon had been considerably improved by Sung times, notably by the addition of sights for aiming and stirrups to aid in drawing. The repeating crossbow, probably first used by the Sung, could discharge bolts at a rate of almost one a second at the cost of reduced accuracy and penetration; it was useful in sieges, but in this period was not as popular as the single-shot type. Large artillery crossbows spanned by winches were in use; but the more common 'light artillery pieces' seem to have been single-armed **stone-throwers** operated by men pulling on ropes. These were used not only in sieges but also in naval warfare, the defence of camps and even in the field, especially for covering river crossings. The rope-operated system, however, was inferior to the true counterweighted trebuchet, introduced by the Yüan, which eventually replaced it.

The aspect of military technology most often associated with China in this period is of course the use of **gunpowder**. Probably invented accidentally by alchemists under the T'ang, gunpowder was first used for fire-arrows and in impregnated fuses for flamethrowers soon after the end of that dynasty. The flamethrower, a borrowing from the Byzantines, was common in naval and siege warfare from that time on; and by the 11th century the Sung were using explosive bombs thrown from siege engines. The Mongols were terrified by these weapons when they first met them in China, but by Kubilai's time had adopted them from the Kin and were using them against the Sung. Bombs with metal casings, which burst to scatter lethal splinters, were now common, a famous illustration of one appearing on the Japanese *Mongol Invasion Scroll* of 1293 (see MAA 105, *The Mongols*). These were mass-produced in tens of thousands and were made in a variety of sizes, ranging from enormous bombs which had to be hauled by draught animals to grenades which could be thrown by hand. The Ming sometimes strapped them to oxen which were driven into an enemy camp. The same technology also gave rise to defensive mines, made from lengths of bamboo filled with powder, which by the late 14th century could be buried under gates and at frontier passes and exploded by a tripwire attached to a flint-and-steel detonator.

More significant for the future were two types of artillery developed under the Yüan – the true gun and the **rocket**. Although the latter was invented about the 11th century there seems to be no firm evidence for its use in war by the Sung, who used the term later used for rockets to denote fire-arrows. Battle accounts start to mention rockets in the 1340s, and multiple launchers may have first appeared in the civil war of 1399–1402. Explosive warheads were not used, the missiles being no more than small rocket-propelled arrows, but a wheeled launcher could fire several hundred at once. They were placed in holes in wooden frames, drilled at an angle to increase dispersion; inaccuracy was considered an advantage, as while their approach could be seen from a distance their eventual point of impact was unpredictable, and this had a demoralising effect on enemy units over a wide front.

Often carried on wheelbarrows, the launchers were mobile enough to be used widely in battles as well as sieges. Smaller versions could be carried by individual men, massed into a bodyguard or dispersed for surprise among conventionally armed troops; but had to be fired within range of enemy

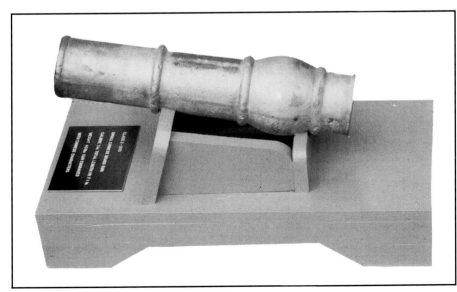

Bronze gun found in Mongolia and dated by the inscription to the year 1409. This was probably left behind by one of the Yung Lo Emperor's northern expeditions. (By permission of the Royal Artillery Historical Trust)

archery, which is no doubt why drawings generally show their users as heavily armoured. Extreme range for the larger launchers, however, may have been well in excess of 500 paces. The *Huo Lung Ching* describes a number of ambitious attempts to improve rocket technology, including multi-stage rockets, a device shaped like a bird and carrying a bomb for use against ships and encampments, and one which ignited a second rocket as it burned out, and flew back to the launcher after dropping a bomb. It is hard to believe that these were ever successfully used in battle, and in fact the use of rockets declined in the 16th century when modern guns became available, testifying to their lack of killing power. Long before this the explosive bombs thrown by trebuchets had apparently fallen into disuse.

Development of the true gun

The true **gun** had its roots in a 10th-century invention, the 'huo-ch'iang' or 'fire-lance', which was originally no more than a firework tied to a spear but by 1260 was evolving into a variety of types, still usually incorporating some sort of blade but shooting out smoke, small projectiles or even poison along with the flames. These weapons were particularly associated with peasant rebels but were also adopted by regular Sung troops, who took them into Yüan service. They had a range of only a few feet and so were basically close-combat weapons, but were cheap to make and remained popular until well after the Ming period, sometimes being combined in mobile racks for the defence of cities. Fire-lances were in use for centuries before the two advances were made which would lead to their evolution into effective firearms – the development of a formula for gunpowder which gave the necessary explosive force, and the use of projectiles fitting the bore of the weapon which could be propelled with sufficient force to kill.

Because this was an evolutionary process it is difficult to fix an exact date for the invention of the true gun, but Needham (see Bibliography) has identified a bronze handgun from Manchuria as dating from Kubilai's expedition of 1287–1288, and believes that their first appearance may have been around 1250. The earliest definitely dated cannon, an example in the National Historical Museum in Peking, is ascribed to the year 1332. These dates are not much earlier than the first firearms in Europe and the Middle East, but the fact that both the weapons and the formulae for gunpowder which appeared in Europe in the first decades of the 14th century are identical to Chinese types, and show no prior history of experimentation and development in the West, strongly suggests that they were transmitted from Yüan China.

The early Ming saw the appearance of new types of firearm, perhaps developed secretly under the Yüan in preparation for revolt. The *Ming Shih* claims that guns were first acquired by the dynasty from Annam in 1410, but other evidence disproves this. In fact the *Huo Lung Ching* states that they were an important factor in the Ming victory over its rivals. The later Yüan, however, also possessed both handguns and heavier pieces, as did the rival warlord Chang Shih-cheng; the commander in 1356 of the first Ming unit of handgunners was a defector from the Yüan army, where he had learned his skills.

Surviving 14th-century guns are usually of bronze, although cast iron was also used; they generally have bulbous, thickened breeches and flared muzzles like contemporary European weapons, and were designed to fire arrows, metal or stone balls, or case shot consisting of up to a hundred small pellets in a bag. By the 15th century thick metal bands were being cast on barrels to strengthen them, again paralleling developments in Europe. Despite the enthusiasm of the manuals and other contemporary writings, however, there is reason to believe that Chinese firearms were fairly unsatisfactory, and accidents with gunpowder were very common. A 15th-century writer, Ch'iu Chun, remarks on the guns' very low rate of fire, enabling an enemy to overrun them before they could reload. Handgunners were therefore deployed in groups of five: one or two to shoot, and the rest to help with loading. Hardwood guns firing arrows were brought back from Annam in 1410 and regarded as superior to Chinese weapons, as were European types when introduced in the 16th century – in fact the latter replaced traditional guns and rockets within a surprisingly short time.

After about 1400 Chinese military technology began to stagnate – a consequence of the low social status of soldiers, the lack of sophisticated enemies to stimulate development, and the suspicion with which Emperors in the Hung Wu tradition regarded innovations, especially those which might weaken the

The restored Ming fortifications of Sian, a city frequently exposed to Mongol raids. (Duncan Head)

power of the state. Although in Europe gunpowder strengthened royal control by enabling governments to destroy the castles of the nobility, in China it tended instead to aid the defence; the enormous thickness of rammed earth fortifications resisted cannon fire in a way which the vertical stone walls of contemporary Europe could not.

There was a great deal of continuity throughout the period in **armour** construction; illustrations from the 1620s show armour and helmets identical to those in paintings of the Sung era and even before. Lamellar, constructed of laced iron or leather plates, already had a long history in China when the Mongols introduced their own versions, and although surviving sets are much later there is no reason to doubt that it remained popular under the Ming. Chinese versions, however, were generally inferior to armours made in Central Asia or Tibet, and in 1374 the Hung Wu Emperor had to introduce regulations to improve their manufacture, insisting for example that they were laced with leather thongs rather than cord. Such armour was often protected with a coat of red or black lacquer. A more distinctively Chinese type of protection was brigandine, of riveted plates covered with fabric. Mail was used only by the western guard units of the Yüan. To judge from illustrations the majority of infantrymen did not wear armour, although it may sometimes have been hidden under robes. Horsemen were generally better protected and horse armour was known, but probably used only by a minority of cavalry.

STRATEGY AND TACTICS

The ancient Chinese tradition of the art of war, dating back to the Chou dynasty, was still very much alive; one of the classical commentators on the *Sun Tzu*, Liu Chi, was an advisor to Chu Yuan-chang. The manuals which survive represent only a fraction of the body of writing on military affairs available to the commanders of the period: a Sung bibliography lists 347 such works, of which only two are now extant.

Strategy was often fairly ambitious, involving e.g. the converging attacks by widely separated forces which were sent against Lin-an in 1276 and K'aifeng in 1368; equally impressive are the distances covered by expeditions across difficult terrain, whether the mountains of Szechwan in the Ta-li campaign of 1251, the Burmese jungle or the Gobi desert in Mongolia. Supply was no doubt made easier by Chinese road-building skills and by the excellent road network which existed within the Empire. Large numbers of bridges also facilitated river crossings. In 1484 an attempt was made to improve the mobility of the infantry on the northern frontier by carrying them in carts, but this was not successful.

Battlefield tactics emphasised surprise, either through deceptions such as the use of smoke or dummies on horseback, or by manoeuvring independent divisions against the enemy's flank or rear; Ming armies usually consisted of three or five such divisions, controlled by a system of signal flags. When fighting Mongols the main problem was to prevent them using their superior mobility to avoid battle or to escape from pursuit if defeated. This was overcome by swift surprise raids on their encampments, or by trying to force them to give battle with their backs to an obstacle, as happened at Lake Buyur in 1388.

At the level of individual unit tactics, however, little subtlety was in evidence. Infantry attacks took the form of wild charges, the men making faces and screaming to frighten the enemy and accompanied by as much noise as possible from drums, gongs and trumpets. The natural indiscipline of the troops was made worse by the practice of rewarding them for taking heads, making it difficult to rally them after a victory. It seems that when necessary missile troops took cover behind those armed with spears and halberds, but the *Wu Ching Tsung Yao* recommends that crossbowmen are deployed separately, and claims that they could defeat a cavalry charge by firepower alone – although in fact resisting cavalry was never a strong suit of Chinese infantry. Crossbowmen used a circulating formation to compensate for their low rate of fire, with men advancing to shoot and retiring to reload. In terms of equipment and tactics it was probably often difficult to tell Chinese cavalry from Mongols, so closely were nomad methods copied; most cavalry thus fought as mounted archers, especially in the north, although this need not imply exclusively skirmishing tactics.

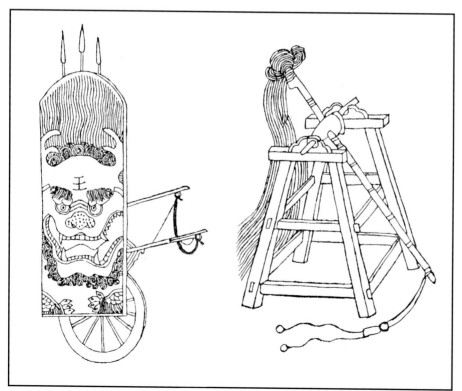

Siege equipment from Wu Pei Chih; *a mobile pavise (left) and a rope-operated engine of a type obsolescent by Ming times.* Huo Lung Ching *describes the use in open battle of wheelbarrow-mounted pavises, carrying fire-lances and accompanied by swordsmen.*

Most Mongol battles were won by hand-to-hand fighting after an initial softening up with arrows, and Ming cavalry are recorded as making impetuous charges, as at Hsin-ch'eng in 1365. Against Nayan in 1287 Kubilai strengthened his cavalry with units of Chinese infantry carried behind their saddles, who dismounted to attack the horses of the enemy.

An army forced onto the defensive generally made use of field fortifications, as at Ting-hsi in 1370 when part of the Ming line was protected by a stream and the rest by palisades. The techniques available for fortifying camps were very sophisticated and often involved the use of artillery. Siege warfare was also highly developed, although defensive techniques were neglected under the Yüan. City walls were of rammed earth, sometimes faced with stone, and overlooked by high towers. Large central towers were also built inside the walls of major towns. These walls, especially when protected with layers of rope matting or clay, could absorb the impact of missiles and so were seldom breached, although rebels took Nan-ch'ang in 1362 by destroying a gate with cannon fire. Blockade, assault and mining were more usually successful techniques. Gunpowder weapons were popular for the defence of towns, in which role they were more effective than in the field; in beating off an assault on Tung-ch'ang by the Prince of Yen in 1400, for example, they are said to have caused tens of thousands of casualties, including a number of generals.

SIX SIGNIFICANT BATTLES

The following battles have been selected as illustrating particular aspects of the military system in action.

Hsiang-yang and Fanch'eng, 1268–1272

These two cities, situated on either side of the Han River, were garrisoned by the Sung to prevent the Mongols advancing downriver to the Yangtze. Initially the Yüan forces, including thousands of Chinese levies, attempted to blockade the cities by patrolling the river and building siegeworks; but although the Sung failed in several break-out attempts the blockade was not close enough to prevent supplies getting through. Two Sung officers, Chang Shun and Chang Kuei, led a flotilla of boats to break in and reprovision Hsiang-yang, an operation which was successful despite the deaths of both leaders.

The Sung commander, Lu Wen-huan, showed no sign of giving up after four years of siege. Kubilai therefore employed two Muslim engineers, sent from Persia by his nephew Abakha, who built large counterweight stone-throwing engines of a type not previously seen in China. With these they bombarded Fanch'eng with rocks and explosive bombs, leading to a successful assault. Turned against Hsiang-yang, one of the engines wrecked the central tower of the city and the garrison surrendered. Marco Polo in his account attempts to take the credit for the construction of these devices, but Chinese sources make it clear that the engineers were Iraqis. The Arab type of counterweighted trebuchet was henceforth known in China as the 'Hui-hui p'ao' or 'Muslim engine', or as the 'Hsiang-yang p'ao'.

Lung-wan, 1360

Ch'en Yu-liang of Han attempted to sail his fleet up the San-ch'a River, a tributary of the Yangtze, and take Chin-ling from Ming troops by surprise. Finding his way blocked by a stone bridge and the river banks covered with sharpened stakes to deter a landing, he returned to the mouth of the river and built a fortified camp. Chu Yuan-chang of the Ming had anticipated this, and devised a plan to lure him out. Chu himself took up a position in front of Ch'en's camp with a third of his army, deploying a flanking force under Ch'ang Yu-ch'un behind a range of hills; he then led an attack on the fortifications. As expected, the Han, seeing an inferior force attacking them, sallied out to eliminate it, whereupon Chu hoisted a yellow flag. At this signal Ch'ang charged into the flank of the enemy and routed them: 20,000 Han were killed and 7,000 captured. Meanwhile the tide had gone out and stranded the Han fleet in the mud; hundreds of ships, soon to form the core of a Ming fleet, were taken.

Ch'u-t'ang Gorge, 1371

The state of Shu in the western province of Szechwan built a defensive position across one of the great Yangtze gorges to stop the advance of a Ming river fleet under Liao Yung-chung. Iron chain booms were stretched across the river to obstruct the ships, while between the cliffs on both banks were three suspension bridges sited to command the booms with fire. On the bridges and on both banks the Shu deployed artillery, probably stone-throwing trebuchets but possibly including cannon. A Ming attempt to break through was repulsed; so Liao landed a detachment of infantry, who wore green clothing and cloaks made of leaves for camouflage as the banks were thickly wooded. These men worked their way round the Shu position and attacked it from behind, while cannon on the Ming ships fired at the bridges – a tactic which suggests a high-trajectory weapon like a mortar. The bridges were destroyed, and Liao's ships, their bows armoured with iron, broke through the chains and forced the position.

T'u-mu, 1449

The Cheng-t'ung Emperor led an expedition against the Oirat Mongols, giving military command to Wang Chen. The army, which included the whole of the 'Ching-wei', was said to number 500,000, and the Mongols characteristically fell back before it into the steppe. The march was slowed by heavy rain, and when the army reached Yang-ho only to find the corpses of a Ming force massacred by the enemy Wang decided to retire, claiming a victory. The Mongols closed in behind them, wiped out a rearguard and ambushed a cavalry force sent to rescue it. At T'u-mu, eight miles short of the walled town of Huai Lai, Wang ordered a halt, refusing to press on, although the site was waterless, for fear of having to abandon the baggage train. The next day the camp was surrounded by 20,000 Mongols, who promised to spare the lives of the troops if they threw down their arms. Made desperate by thirst, many did so, and the army disintegrated as they ran in disorder towards a nearby river. The Mongols slaughtered them and captured the Emperor.

Ta-t'eng hsia, 1466

The rebellious Yao and Chuang tribes of Kwangsi in south-west China assembled in the Ta-t'eng hsia Gorge on the Ch'ien River, a steep ravine flanked by jungle-clad mountains. A Ming force under Han Yung, consisting of 160,000 local levies and 30,000 regular soldiers including 1,000 Mongols, was sent to blockade the mouth of the gorge, but ordered not to risk an attack. Han ignored both his orders and local advice and entered the ravine, where the Yao resisted from behind a series of wooden stockades. At first unsuccessful, Han resorted to setting fire to the stockades with incendiary missiles and then storming them. The Yao fled and were massacred, while many of the Chuang, who were deadly archers renowned for their use of poisoned arrows, surrendered and were recruited into the government forces. They were then used to occupy the gorge, denying it to the rebels.

Hung-yen-ch'ih, 1473

Wang Yueh, a scholar by training, devised a policy of striking back at the Mongols by adopting their own tactics. He led 4,600 horse-archers, equipped like nomads, into the steppes north of Ning-hsia. At Hung-yen-ch'ih he surprised the camp of Bag Arslan's Mongols while the warriors were away raiding, overwhelmed the few guards and captured many horses and other livestock. Bag Arslan learned of this and rode back in haste, but fell into an ambush laid by Wang. The tribesmen were decisively defeated and retreated to the north-west.

Suggested reading:
The Cambridge History of China, Vol. 7, Part 1; Cambridge University Press, 1988.
A. Chan, *The Glory and Fall of the Ming Dynasty*; University of Oklahoma Press, 1982.
C. C. Hsiao, *The Military Establishment of the Yüan Dynasty*; Harvard University Press, 1978.
F. Kierman and J. Fairbank, *Chinese Ways in Warfare*; Harvard University Press, 1974.
J. Needham, *Science and Civilisation in China*; Cambridge University Press – especially Vol. 5, Part 7, 'The Gunpowder Epic', 1989.
Marco Polo, *The Travels*; Penguin Classics edition, trans. R. Latham, 1958.
M. Rossabi, *Khubilai Khan*; London, 1988.
H. Russell Robinson, *Oriental Armour*; Herbert Jenkins, 1967.
B. Smith and W. G. Weng, *China: A History in Art*; New York, 1972.

A watchtower on the Great Wall in Inner Mongolia. Although later than our period this illustrates the type of border fortification which was emerging in the 15th century. (Mrs. G. Piercey)

A. Waldron, *The Great Wall of China*; Cambridge University Press, 1990.
See also the chapter on Kubilai in D. Nicolle, *The Mongol Warlords*; Firebird Books, 1990. Numerous other works on the Mongols contain useful information on Yüan China.

THE PLATES

A: Cavalry of the Yüan period, c.1260

This encounter between a Chinese and a Mongol cavalryman illustrates examples of the respective armour styles of the two peoples. Either, however, could be found fighting for or against the Yüan or even the Ming.

A1: Mongol heavy cavalryman

Based on an early Ming painting depicting nomad horsemen, this man wears armour of iron lamellae in a style popular in Asia for centuries. The horse armour is of similar construction but of lacquered leather; leather armour was more common than iron, and a Khitan source implies that only the strongest horses could bear the weight of metal protection. Most Mongols would be unarmoured, resembling

Plate D1. This warrior's weapons are a composite bow about five feet long, carried strung in a case, and a sabre. A minority of Mongols would also carry lances. See MAA 105, *The Mongols*, for reconstructions of other Mongol troops of this period.

A2: Chinese cavalryman

This figure's armour and horse furniture are based on illustrations in *Wu Pei Chih*, but represent a tradition dating back to the T'ang. The fabric covering of the armour conceals riveted iron plates. Shoulder pieces like those of E2 could be added; but neither this man nor his opponent carries a shield. Cavalry shields are described in manuals as round and made of ox-hide, but are rarely shown in art and were probably not widely used in East Asia. The weapon is a 'li hua ch'iang' or 'pear-flower spear', a primitive form of fire-lance. This was a popular weapon in Sung China and is described in use by cavalry at the siege of Yangchow in 1276.

B: Chinese troops of the Yüan, c.1280
B1: Guardsman

Based on a Sung figurine in the British Museum, this man wears a long robe and soft cap, and probably represents a soldier on palace guard duty. The original is armed only with a sword, the axe being

Statue of a Ming official from the processional way at Peking. This form of *headgear was worn by courtiers in civilian dress. (Rev. P. Ward)*

taken from a Ming manual. His hands, like those of the other figures in this plate, have been tattooed: this was standard practice under the Sung as a precaution against desertion, and although the Yüan discontinued it many of their 'Hsin-fu' troops retained this distinguishing feature. Guardsmen could also be tattooed on their faces.

B2: Crossbowman

This soldier wears the typical dress of the ordinary Chinese infantryman, closely based on the working costume of the peasantry except for the boots, a mark of a military man. Black and white were the colours prescribed for commoners by Sung law, but by Yüan times this system of denoting rank by clothing colour was generally ignored. However, the Chinese still distinguished themselves from the 'barbarians' by their dress, particularly by the wearing of hats and belts, and the fastening of garments from left to right. He is armed with a repeating crossbow, reconstructed from a modern example, which was operated by a lever which cocked the bow and caused the bolts to drop from a magazine on top. It was probably still a rarity at this date.

B3: Infantryman

Although his tattoos mark him out as having served the Sung, this man is probably a 'Han jen' or northerner, and is based on a tomb figure of the Yüan period from Shansi. His long robe and broad-brimmed hat were often associated with servants, but the long hair was a symbol of courage worn by soldiers. He is carrying a halberd from *Wu Pei Chih*.

C: Southern auxiliaries of the Yüan, c.1300
C1: Fukienese tribesman

Marco Polo describes some of the exotic tribesmen of southern China who were subjects of Kubilai Khan. The men of 'Fu-chau' fought on foot with swords and spears, and are described as bloodthirsty cannibals. Polo gives no information on shields, that carried by this man being based on those used by Yüan auxiliaries on the Japanese *Mongol Invasion Scroll*. These are often regarded as Korean, but are just as likely to come from the Chinese coastal provinces.

C2: Military official

This figure, reconstructed from a statuette from the same source as B3, combines the stiff cap of a bureaucrat with military boots. The cummerbund around his waist was a common feature of Chinese costume; compare the stiff waist protector worn by A2. The official is almost certainly not legally entitled to his elaborate purple robe. Officers were issued with gold or silver tablets, decorated with pearls, as symbols of rank.

C3: Southern pirate

Conscripted salt-smugglers and pirates were a major source of manpower for the Yüan in south China. The clumsy-looking armour is made from several layers of paper stuffed with cotton, a type of protection which was light and virtually arrow-proof. It would not be practical for marching long distances, but was popular with sailors and garrison troops. His weapon is an advanced type of fire-lance, favoured for repelling boarders from ships.

D: The Red Turban Revolt, c.1350
D1: Mongol Trooper

A Ming dynasty painting in the Victoria and Albert Museum shows a Mongol in this costume, better adapted to the humid summers of Central China than the traditional furs. The decrees of Ming Emperors ordering their Mongol subjects to adopt Chinese dress were not entirely successful. The horse-furniture, decorated with red tassels, is very similar to the style used by Ming cavalry.

D2: Red Turban rebel

The Red Turbans would have differed at first from the mass of the peasantry only by their adoption of distinguishing red headgear. This man is unarmed, and has to rely on the martial arts techniques disseminated by the secret societies. Some authorities believe that the high kicks for which northern Chinese unarmed combat styles are famous were originally developed as a counter to Mongol cavalry, who rode with very short stirrups and so were easily unseated by a hard blow, while being less able to take evasive action than would be a target on foot.

E: Ming troops, c.1400
E1: Halberdier

Based on drawings in *Wu Pei Chih*, this figure is probably typical of the infantry of the 14th to 17th centuries. The long shield, one of several variants on this basic shape, has been crudely painted in an attempt at psychological warfare. Another example of this sort of approach is the tassel attached to the halberd blade, designed to distract an opponent as he tried to parry a blow. It is not clear whether such troops would wear soft hats or helmets; the plume often illustrated suggests the latter, but surviving examples are lacking.

E2: Standard bearer

This man wears a helmet and body armour of traditional type, as illustrated in *Wu Pei Chih* and in art as early as the Sung. The wearing of a small flag fixed to the helmet was probably in origin a Chinese practice which spread via the Mongols to the Middle East (and was not unknown in the West). Ming armies were accompanied by enormous numbers of

flags, both for communication purposes and to raise morale while intimidating the enemy. The characters on this flag read 'Tai Ming', 'Great Brilliance', the slogan of the dynasty.

E3: Handgunner

Illustrations show gunners in this type of long robe, which may conceal armour, despite its seeming unsuitability for a man who had to work in proximity to lighted matches. Most surviving guns are, like this one, of cast bronze, and the small size is typical; they were, however, fairly heavy because of the thickness of the metal. Ignition was via a small touch-hole on the top, the serpentine lever not being introduced into China until the 16th century. Drawings commonly show no provision for carrying powder and shot, but we may assume that a bag or box would be used for this purpose, perhaps removed to a safe distance before the gun was fired. Even in the 16th century Chinese troops are described as clumsy in

Chinese or Tibetan helmet, early 15th century. Helmets constructed of overlapping iron plates were a common alternative to the one-piece bowl, but this example is unique in the number of plates used; eight or fewer would be more usual. (The Board of Trustees of the Royal Armouries no. XXVIA. 150)

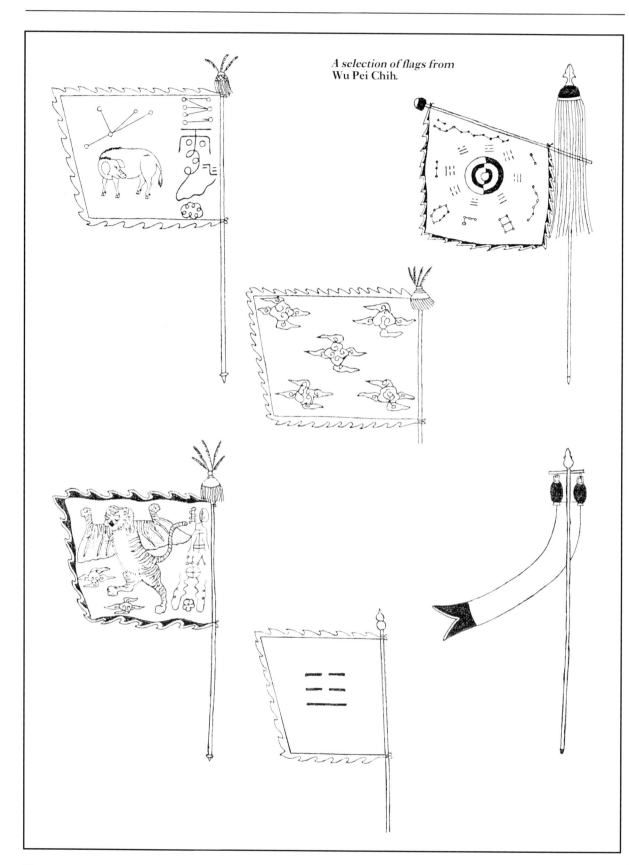

A selection of flags from Wu Pei Chih.

their handling of gunpowder, often injuring themselves through unfamiliarity or carelessness.

F: Rocket-launcher, c.1450

One of the most ingenious uses ever devised for the wheelbarrow – itself a Chinese invention – was as a mobile rocket-launcher. This plate is based on a reconstructed scale model in the National Historical Museum in Peking, and on the *Wu Pei Chih*. Six box launchers were carried, four on the top row and two below; hundreds of rockets could thus be fired in a few seconds. Note the guns and spear blades fixed to the frame, and the apron which could be let down at the front to protect the crew. Two artillerymen were employed to fire the rockets, which were ignited by fuses protruding from each box, and two labourers pushed the barrow. The wearing on uniforms of patches bearing written characters was probably introduced by the Ming.

G: Ming élite troops, c.1500
G1: Cavalry trooper

Soldiers apparently shown unarmoured in art may have worn coats of brigandine or lamellar armour under their robes. This man is armed with a spear from *Wu Pei Chih*, but could add or substitute a bow of Mongol type. Rewards and promotion were offered in exchange for severed heads, which were graded according to the supposed quality of the enemy: first, Mongols and Manchus; then Tibetans; thirdly, the aboriginal tribes of the south-west; and finally Chinese rebels.

G2: Rocketeer

This man's coat of leather lamellae is based on a Manchu period example in the Tower of London, but its close similarity to Mongol styles shows the survival of a long tradition right through our period. The hand-held rocket launcher is illustrated in several manuals from the 15th century onwards. It could be carried and fired by one man, but had an effective range of less than 200 paces. They were used in very large numbers; the garrison of Hsuan-fu in 1449, for example, had 90,000 rockets available.

G3, G4: Drummers

Drums, gongs, cymbals and trumpets were an important part of warfare in the Ming period; like the flags, they had a psychological as well as a communications function. These men wear typical infantry dress as shown in *Wu Pei Chih*.

H: Ming commander and staff, c.1500
H1: Civilian official

The Ming army was plagued by numerous civil servants intended to supervise the generals and ensure their loyalty. This figure is based on an 18th-century painting, but wears the traditional long robe and soft cap of the scholar class.

H2: Ming general

Flanking the road to the tombs of the Ming Emperors outside Peking are several statues of high-ranking officers, on which this figure is based. His elaborate armour shows many of the distinguishing features of Chinese styles of the period, and similarities between it and the equipment of A2 are obvious. The basic construction is of small iron plates, supplemented by lamellar forearm defences and helmet aventail. The short cloak around the shoulders is a common feature. Substituted here for the original sword is a Japanese weapon, suspended in 'tachi' style from the belt: during the 15th century, China began to import these excellent swords for the use of officers wealthy enough to afford them.

H3: Standard bearer

The flag accompanying the general bears the character 'ling', signifying command. The ancient Chou system of divisional flags was still in use: this indicated the right wing by a flag bearing a white tiger, the left by a green dragon, the vanguard by a red bird, the rearguard by a black tortoise, and the commander-in-chief by the Great Bear constellation. *Wu Pei Chih* illustrates a variety of other designs including animals, trigrams and zodiacal signs.

Notes sur les planches en couleur

Les styles d'armure des cavaliers chinois et mongols
A1 L'armure à lamelles de fer. Armure de cheval en cuir laqué. Les armes sont des sabres et des arcs composés, d'une longueur de 5 pieds, qu'on porte dans un étui. **A2** L'armure est couverte d'un tissu pour protéger les plaques de fer rivées. Cette arme est un 'Li hua chiang' ou 'lance à fleur de poire', la forme primitive de la lance de feu.

B1 La robe longue et le calot mou représentent le soldat en service de garde au palais. Le tatouage à la main est une précaution contre la désertion **B2** Tenue typique du fantassin chinois ordinaire, basé de très près sur le costume de travail des paysans, ceci apart les bottes qui sont la marque de l'homme militaire. Armé d'une arbalète à répétition opérée par un levier qui arme l'arc de sorte que les carreaux soient largués d'un magasin sur le dessus. **B3** On associe la robe longue et le chapeau à bord large avec les domestiques mais les cheveux longs signifient le courage chez les soldats. Il porte une hallebarde de 'Wu Pei Chih'.

C1 Le bouclier porté par cet homme est basé sur ceux utilisés par les auxiliaires Yüan sur le 'Mongol Invasion Scroll' japonais. **C2** Le calot rigide d'un bureaucrate qui porte des bottes militaires. La ceinture autour de la taille est un détail fréquent chez les chinois. **C3** L'armure peu maniable est fabriquée à partir de plusieurs couches de papier bourrées avec du coton.

D1 Ce costume mongol est mieux adapté aux étés humides de la Chine Centrale que les fourrures traditionnelles. Les équipements des chevaux sont décorés de glands, semblables à ceux utilisés par la cavalrie Ming. **D2** On peut distinguer les 'Turbans Roues' par les couvre-chefs rouges. Ils ne sont pas armés.

E1 Probablement typique à l'infantrie des 14è et 17è siècles. Le bouclier est peint imparfaitement, des glands sont attachés à la lame de la hallebarde. La plume suggère que ces soldats portent des casques. **E2** Le casque et l'armure tenu dans le style traditionnel et on aperçoit un petit drapeau sur le casque. **E3** Ce fusil est petit mais lourd, vu qu'il est de bronze, et on n'aperçoit pas de provision pour la poudre ni le plomb; de longues robes.

F Lance-fusée mobile. Les lames de fusil et de lance sont fixés au cadre et on laisse tomber une couverture pour protéger l'équipage.

G1 Armé d'une lance. Ne sont pas armés mais auraient peut-être porté les manteaux en brigadine ou l'armure à lamelles sous la robe. **G2** Manteau à lamelles en cuir, basé sur l'exemple de l'époque mandchou. Le lanceur de fusée est tenu à la main et peut être porté et tiré par un seul homme. **G3, G4** Des tambours, gongs, cymbales et trompettes. Des hommes qui portent la tenue typique de l'infantrie.

H1 Celui-ci porte la longue robe traditionnelle et le calot mou de la classe étudiante. **H2** La construction est faite de petites plaques de fer, avec en plus des défenses en lamelles aux avant bras, puis un cache sur le casque. On porte souvent des capes autour des épaules. Arme japonaise attachée à la ceinture de style 'tachi'. **H3** Le drapeau qui accompagne le général porte le caractère 'ling' qui symbolise son commandement.

Farbtafeln

A Die Rüstungstypen eines chinesischen und eines mongolischen Reiters. **A1** Eine EisenlamellenßRüstung. Pferdepanzer aus lackiertem Leder. Die Waffen bestehen aus einem Verbundbogen, etwa 1,50m lang, schon gespannt in einem Behälter getragen, und aus einem Säbel. **A2** Die Stoffebspannung der Rüstung verdeckt genietete Eisenplatten. Bei der Waffe hanelt es sich um einen 'Li hua ch'ang' oder 'BirnenblütenßSpeer', die primitve Form einer Feuerlanze.

B1 Das lange Gewand und die weiche Kappe bezeichnen wahrscheinlich einen Soldaten der Palastwache. Die Hand ist zur Verhütung des Desertierens tättowiert. **B2** Typische Kleidung des gewöhnlichen chinesischen Infanteristen, eng beruhend auf der Arbeitskleidung der Bauern, mit Ausnhme der Stiefel, die den Soldaten erkennen lassen. Ausgerüstet mit einer Repetier-Armbrust, bedient durch einen Hebel, der den Bogen spannt und die Bolzen von einem oben liegenden Magazin in die Rille fallen läßt. **B3** Langes Gewand und breitkrämpiger Hut sind normalerweise Kennzeichen von Bediensteten, aber das lange Haar ist ein Symbol der Tapferkeit und wird von Soldaten getragen. Er ist mit einer Hellebarde von 'Wu Pei Chih' ausgerüstet.

C1 Der Schild dieses Mannes beruht auf denen der Hilfstruppen in der Abbildung der japanischen 'Schriftrolle der mongolischen Invasion'. **C2** Steife Kappe eines Beamten, der Militärstiefel trägt. Der Kummerbund um die Hüften findet sich häufig bei chinesischen Kostümen. **C3** Plump aussehende Rüstung, bestehend aus mehreren Lagen Papier, mit Baumwolle ausgestopft.

D1 Dieses mongolische Kostüm ist den feuchten Sommern zentralchinas besser angepaßt als die traditionellen Pelze. Pferdeschutz geschmückt mit roten Quasten, ähnlich im Stil wie bei der Ming-Reiterei. **D2** Die roten Turbane als auffallende Kopfbedeckung. Unbewaffnet.

E1 Wahrscheinlich typisch für das Fußvolk des 14. bis zum 17 Jahrhundert. Der lange Schild ist roh bemalt, die Hellebardenklinge ist von einer Quaste geschmückt. Die Feder scheint anzudeuten, daß diese Soldaten Helme trugen. **E2** Helm und Rüstung nach traditioneller Art, mit kleiner Flagge am Helm. **E3** Kleine, aber schwer gegossenen Bronzekanone, ohne Vorkehrngen für die Beförderung von Pulver und Projektilen; lange Gewänder.

F1 Fahrbarer Raketenwerfer. Kanone und Speerblätter am Rahmen befestigt; Schirm konnte vorne gesenkt werden, um die Bedienungsmannschaft zu schützen.

G1 Mit einem Speer bewaffnet. Ungepanzert, könnten aber ein Schuppen- oder Lamellenpanzerhemd unter dem Gewand getragen haben. **G2** Lederlamellenjacke, beruhend auf einem Muster aus der Manchuperiode. Der handgehaltene Raketenwerfer konnte von einem Mann getragen und abgefeuert werden. **G3, G4** Trommeln, Gongs, Zymbeln und Trompeten. Männer in typischer Infanterieuniform.

H1 Trägt traditionelles Gewand und weiche Kappe der Gelehrtenklasse. **H2** Grundlegende Konstruktion bsteht aus kleinen Eisenplatten, ergänzt durch lamellare Unterarmschützer und Helmhalsberge. Kurzer Mantel um die Schultern ist typisch. Japanische Waffe, hängt im 'Tachi'-Stil vom Gürtel. **H3** Die Flagge des Generals trägt das Schriftzeichen 'Ling', was soviel wie Kommando bezeichnet.